**ALIQUOT**

John Clegg was born in Chester in
1986, and grew up in Cambridge. In
2013, he won an Eric Gregory Award.
He works as a bookseller in London.

A GENE SEQUENCE LATER RETITLED

# *Aliquot*

John Clegg

CARCANET POETRY

First published in Great Britain in 2022 by
Carcanet
Alliance House, 30 Cross Street
Manchester, M2 7AQ
www.carcanet.co.uk

A CIP catalogue record for this book is
available from the British Library.

ISBN  978 1 80017 235 7

Book design by Andrew Latimer
Printed in Great Britain by SRP Ltd, Exeter, Devon

The publisher acknowledges financial
assistance from Arts Council England.

CONTENTS

for Annick

When the clock strikes thirteen, doubt is not only cast on the last stroke but also on all that have come before. When the clock strikes fourteen, we throw away the clock.

Thorndike, 1968

## THE LECTURE NOTES

On their way home through the springy fen
one of the pilgrims said: Perhaps the *second*
old man was the real wizard.
                              So the Clerk
unhoisted his black sack and fiddled through
the lecture notes, well knowing that he'd drifted off by then.
He had the knack of silent reading
but the other pilgrims hung so close
to every flicker of his lower lip
for some word which might unmake their bad bargain.

No hope came.
Their packmules sank into the verges gradually.
The Clerk fell like a dolloped stone
through strata of transcendence
till he came to rest on that damp territory yclept
– he checked his notes – yclept, that can't be right, *The Hall of Swindle*.

## ALIQUOT

I have watched for a moment, through the basement
window of the Catering School, attention
paid by the Master as her student
scoops a goodsize helping of green peas
from an institutional aluminium
trough, the deep rectangular kind
that rests in a bain marie, and conveys them
into another trough of the same kind, itself filled
two thirds of the way to its brim with green peas.

Likewise, from the far end of Chalk Farm platform
I have seen a tube come in: in the first
carriage, resting against the backbolster
a woman, resting against her shoulder an uncased cello:
in the first vestibule of the final carriage
a young man, also keeping a cello upright.
Detached, they must have been, from their respective
orchestras, and coalescing only
in my vantage point, experienced nonetheless.

There is one huge vat in the world overbrimming with green peas,
one great orchestra overflowing with cellists:
when the partitions are lifted momentarily
the fact of partitions seems the ridiculous thing:
then when the tube pulls in, or the student
completes his task to the Master's satisfaction,
they rattle down: and the natural unit
of peas goes back to being the serving,
each orchestra reconvenes in its own allocations.

## PROPANE CALENDAR

Supersize plant can't
Negotiate built road with deftness

Moved at night instead
Through purposeways in corn

Alight with warning, no, for
Comfort of the handler

Who glances up
Sometimes and grins or

What, like leading a barn on a
Leash. A little fog

Collects around its
Trim from his high cab

The driver rasps a hooter
Nothing sleeping stirs

Stage right the second
Juggernaut the dawn comes on

Cervantes ransomed
worked at pissant clerk jobs in Toledo.
His non sword arm wouldn't lift
above the horizontal.

In the roadside dust
he undid and enjoyed a whole white onion.
His saddlebag
of purchase orders,

timber, rope, tar, barrelled
cheese in brine
was being slit apart
by two lunks who had no idea

about the proper way to open saddlebags.
He probably
had some commission somewhere on his person
which would clear things up.

Right after he had finished with the onion.
It clung behind his breath
the way a proverb would,
a double-edged or self-refuting proverb.

## THE SUN BOX

*for Emily*

There is a field somewhere which in forty years
will be the corner of a carpark: yours
will be the bay marked 'Visitor', since you are
in the book, and may proceed directly to reception,
one of several not too unattractive
low white buildings. You are slightly early.
Check in via the mandated ritual, whatever
it may be now, and if there's a sofa
lounge on it, your escort has been called
and will be coming presently
                                    to walk you through
what might remind you of an out-of-term-time
science campus – cafe not much used, odd clumps
of postdocs, glimpsed through toughened glass
summer-school students tending spindly arcana –
until you come to what you've come to see,
the small domestic sun suspended buzzing
in the centre of whichever room
from outside seemed most nondescript. My guess is
it will be a disappointment, shielded
in something opaque, offwhite and embossed
with manufacturer's logo, something you are asked
to take on trust; inside meanwhile the miracle
goes on, however dull, being a miracle.

This is the best I think that I can offer you
with any hopefulness: if not uninteresting
times at least uninteresting objects:
a tame sun hung from wires, I believe in it,

the fact of boredom buffing like a reservoir
the whole bit; space which I was born to.
And what I wonder will you do with that?

## LULL

Fog condenses in the engine of the plane it's grounded,
underneath the wings saucepans are full of it, an off-
grey film like scum on unstirred whitewash. Prefab
dorms lean either Company or Jungle: Jungle mellow
in the fog, a forced vacation, pleasant cold compress.
In Company they sit chewing their altitude pills,
worry at the road: the Indians who make the road new
weekly won't come down the mountain now. Nobody's
pipes stay lit. At dusk a young accountant
on the airstrip's edge hallooed two dark shapes wrestling.
He had in mind bored college grads. Next morning
in the Mess an old hand set him straight: a jaguar
wrenching a spider monkey's head clean off.
It must have played both figures that you saw.
It's eating all them monkeys gives them monkeyshines.

## THE PUNT GUN

The punt gun's retort always rammed back the duck punt
deep into the sloshy sluice it was parked in

but nothing distinctly fell: what you observed was
some birds (they'd got wise: fewer

rose each week, until you left it a week, then
the whole flock hotfooted it) out of

the flock made a gradual bank down, as though
they'd an eye to a dignified landing,

and flattened against black fen:
Tiger or Scrap would come swimming and fasten

their jaws around plausible
necklines – and till they came close you'd not swear

they'd plucked anything out of the
air, as if anything waited to fall from the air

as the psalmist had sworn to fowl
palmed out of plain air; these ducks had a palmed-off

feel; as if the flock flew with decoys along-
side, and all that the punt gun could hit were the ghost ducks.

## ANCIENT JUNIPER

Lean soil it prefers, fast rockhold.
I watched one outface a storm –
a manor house hotel near Darlington,
first floor bay window of a conference room
chairs stacked along the stone hearth, baby grand
dustcovered, anyone might
wander in there, looking for the gents
then watch a bit: sleet being dragged
plough disc against the moor
at speed of headlights.
Half a field interlude between each crescent.
Really it was it being dusk, grey
dusk, the dusk somehow
participating in the sleet that gave
each pulse the look of dingy steel.
I stood there a while.
Pricked in white you could
make out the line a drystone wall had run down.
At the rough
midpoint the juniper had jemmied up
some stone as windbreak. Now, about my height,
however many hundred years
it bent into the centre of each blade
and seemed to conjure windbreak –
or at least the plough disc
drove straight through it, never bit
or shattered. That exquisite
minimum of flex is what it grows into,
like someone putting on
unhappily a wet shirt, since there's nothing else.

Little inlet, my legitimate
            backwater, low tide
will about bear my front wheel's weight but not quite
            so I make the jolly
Wattwurm jump out of its sandcast
as I visit, four miles off, friend lighthousekeeper.

Lighthousekeeper
            is manouvering
a giant bulb upstairs, but has a candle
burning on his kitchen table
            I keep company.
Friend candle, Herr Wineglass, lost moth,

let's call each other *du*. Mud pools
disintegrate to mist, it is
            an alright night.
I scan a posted crib of signals for 'distress'
in fifty languages, flag language, wind,
            bird language:

            once, a calm day
on the dyke, I watched high overhead a fulmar
being dragged backward by something like a riptide –
            his big
wingtips found no purchase anywhere.
And not a breath of wind at human level!

So my proper lookout is this shallow camber,
coaxing storms into the over-
      or the undercurrents.
Lighthousekeeper, dredge upstairs for souls
      drowning or floundering – I'll
tend below this inlet, wineglass, candle.

Faience pendant anthropoid bust amulet
Findplace unknown
Too fineworked and too small
To be well-clenched

So not among
The small bones of the hand
Reached for in crumpled
Ribs instead
Dust blown off
Held up to the light

Then conveyed
To the faience heap

The superyacht rides off the shore
a little farther from the shore
than normal for the time of year;
the portholes seem
to brush great hanks of wet fringe from their eyes
all through the storm. It would be good,
the captain claims, to broach
the question of the second bottle
with the absent owner
represented by this broom wedged down the chairback
in a yachting cap
and shouldering a dinner jacket,
nope, he's no objection
if we move on to the *Stolichnaya Elit.*
It goes round the skeleton
crew twice and now the sea gets lit.

The sea gets lit by tumbled
flakes of gold leaf through the porthole.
Wind deflects
the echo from the thunderclap,
fuzzy detritus
touches down on deck then gets reswept away.
They draw high card to see who gets the master suite.

## THE OZYMANDIAS PROTOCOL

Boundless and Bare, two detectives,
Investigate who stole the trunk.
They conclude that the limbs were defective
But the sculptor by now's done a bunk.

So they pull in an elderly tourist
To establish the dates of his trip.
He is full of complaints, but seems sorest
That a big head's been giving him lip.

So they question the head, Bare and Boundless,
Sunk in sand, which is deeper than thought.
'Your suspicions are all of them groundless',
It growls. 'All your work's come to naught.

You're welcome to both kiss my sandy ass;
Then God help me you'd better be leaving.
Or you'll find out what pull Ozymandias
Still has, in the land of the living.'

They head back to lost pets and divorces,
Expense accounts which they can pad,
Bent DAs, heiresses with horses
Who have gone to the drink or the bad –

And keep themselves out of antique lands
Where wind blows the dust into devils
Where sculptors mock kings with their weak hands
And where only the sand's on the level.

## 'RADICAL ESSEX'


Between two greenhouses a JCB
is making inroads through a spoil heap of overripe
cucumbers, cab so rain-steeled
the operator's spectre gets redrawn
with every windscreenwiper backsweep:
ghost then gone then ghost:
lane with no verge, fields with no footpath,
when the storm picks up where's there to wait but here?
Low open barn. The white vans stream
regardless through a farm with no
farmhouse, swish down the road and mount a hill
without a vantage point. You watch
their headlights pop against the ridge
like shabby loss, like upward thrusting bubbles.

## AN ATTENDANT

I am moving about on the fifth floor of the Francis
Crick Institute in the week before their 'soft opening'

Nothing further this morning needs to be done
A flotilla of vans is approaching from Mill Hill East

With attuned equipment disassembled as much as poss
With flask after flask of *Drosophila*

*Melanogaster*, fruit flies
Zonked from their trip or waking up from the zonk

You can send them by post transatlantically
Jostled to sleep by the turbulence I am awakening

From a 'soft nap' in an empty lab on the upper floor
Looking around all the stooltops are still

Wrapped in plastic looking down into my hands
I am flicking the bit release catch back and forth on my handdrill

## CONVERGENCE

The fishes were vainglorious already
and queried how the ship fell through them only
against their cursory repertoire of query,
the checklist which ticks over in the pearleye:
tick box for 'food', tick box for 'threat' or 'safety'.
It split and threw its coal up in a flurry;
the coal- and metal-dust resettled slowly,
and in the meantime, every checkbox empty,
the fish moved on to vaguely livelier quarry.
It was much later when the crust grew heavy
that seaworms reached the mirror – silvery,
by that point, only as clear night is silvery.
They'd not even the glimmer of a query.
The fish returned in quiet hunting parties.

## THE HIGH LAMA EXPLAINS HOW ITEMS ARE PROCURED FOR SHANGRI-LA

'Every third decade or so, a convoy of porters –
such as, my major domo informs me, you yourself
once belonged to – receives an unusual commission:

the expedition they are carrying for is to be indefinitely
delayed (you know how easily such an excuse
can be fabricated), and one small item of cargo

is to be lost – a piano, some bannister ends,
a ceremonial urn of the sort you were admiring earlier
in the stairwell, it might be, it might well be –

once this is missing beyond all relocation
the caravan picks up and shambles on: we trust
up here to the natural drift of unmoored objects,

a convoy travelling crossways some years later
ditches a satchel of pillowcases down a crevasse,
a herdsman finds an entire silver service, minus

the fish-knives, stowed under scree on a hillside:
either he leaves them, then creeps back at night
to find them already vanished; or he uses them

all his life and they pass by bequest
up the valley into the blue mountains already mentioned
when we were discussing this place's preciseish location.'

## DORMER WINDOWS

Grid streets in Pardue
Oriented so the sun

May rise on cue in certain
Dormer windows

Are a starmap out of
Kilter with the field lines –

Which justify their own grid
By the gradient

At which cows
Topple in high weather.

Where the grids mesh
Pardue takes priority,

Those fields which abut
Town backlots carve out

Equilateral packages
Of diddly-squat.

Like here. Two cows
Relentlessly chew off the overlay,

Expose the one-
To-one map of the very local.

Houses, being fixed,
Seem transitory:

Impositions on this other grid
Which, though

Imaginary, is our measure
Of the permanent.

Because what can't be filched
Needn't be nailed down.

## FARMER'S RIVIERA

Nobody had insurance
but at the volcano auction held after every eruption
it was good form to bid over value
for any obliterated lots on the flankland.

A local policeman pots hares with his choppy shotgun.
Upslope, new rootstock is being tapped in,
olive and medlar:
propitious, unrealistic.

A ranger in a documentary,
thirty years
in the Sierra de Andújar, foot and horseback,
never seen one.
Went to piss in the wood
and caught her sideeye –
crouched ecstatic, watched for half an hour,
both of them perfectly motionless.
Deer crashed through
and the lynx stayed motionless.
When the ranger investigated
his lynx was a housebrick propped against a treestump.

\*

I sought her in the tractor passing places,
in the mud covert, behind
dispersing mice, in absences
of birdsong or in birdsong undertones.
Startled they don't flinch, I was told,
not like domestic cats,
they haven't options which need weighing up
but make a coil of themselves
then slip that coil.
How to see one: lie down flat
and focus where she isn't.
Earlier that day she might have passed behind you.

# HURRICANE JOAQUIN

When the first notes of the forecast
had fulfilled themselves, the lobby
navigable but the muddy water rising,
those staff who'd elected to remain
at the hotel (seasonal cleaning help
shorthauling in the basement dorm)
began to jerk the mattresses upstairs.
The management, which for the moment
was Clarisse – some nights she deputised
on front-of-house – acquired waders
and made one sweep of the kitchens.
Doubtless there was something salvageable
down there her torch never settled on:
instead she found twelve cheery lobsters
waiting in their tank. No CCTV.
There were doors ajar. She reached in,
chose one, leant it on the tank's lip
long enough to snip the blue twist
from the claw, then stooped into the cold
and when she let it go, whatever urge
possessed her vanished, she returned
to help an optimistic Eritrean girl
move sandbags two stairs further up the staircase.

## JUMP, SCORPION,

between the bars of the bootrack
you were tapped out against, and then again between
chairlegs (our banquet table was set up
far too close to the bootrack):

the prestigious archaeologist
is thrashing his hat at the last
known quadrant of groundsheet you covered –
on your tiptoe, but heart in it.

*(after Stefan Andres)*

## THE CHOPPING BOARD

It felt as though the hotel grew from scratch
around the lumber room, each piece of junk
was wider than the doorframe. Sawing through
a headboard of what must have been the next
size up from kingsize bed I yelled at Pat
to chuck a scrap of wood to wedge it level.
OK it was level. In the afternoon
we sat against the skip, that scrap between us,
somewhere flat to lay a drink; it struck me
that it was or it had been a chopping board,
a dark stain down the centre 'where they laid
the chicken's neck', said Pat, 'or someone
lost their fingertip – you take against
a piece of wood for that. We ought to find
somewhere to hide this back.' What came to mind,
though, was a knife, the burglar's knife I found
in long grass after the police had been
and I was eight or nine. He'd taken ours
to shim the household locks, so I wiped his
against my jeans, no dirt but frost, and opening
the kitchen drawer laid it askew, so who
soever found it next would take it for
our own, and any bad juju or small dis
quiet for the portion they'd brought with them.

## LANGUAGE AS SONORA

A pea-sized seedpod of the creosote bush
Can be germinated artificially in boiling water.
After it's been planted out it needs one
Irrigation to instil in it the memory of water:
Every clone will reprint that initial downpour
As they spill off tendrils from the fading centre.

That was how I thought my daughter's words
Would come, her first perception
Rippling away in tokens: when she spoke,
Though, each rang like a cloudburst:
Not a remnant memory but a xeriscape
Blooming from scratch with every thunderstorm.

## THE BASS BOAT

One gallon water per inch of fish:
he showed me the livewell, and mentioned how
the Department of the Interior
entertained a longrunning suspicion about a particular
panel of perspex under the livewell:
the man who'd sold him the boat had paid off
his boat loan by running dope over
the state line bisecting the lake,
which oddly enough you could actually *see*
some moonlit evenings. But if they drew up
alongside now and asked him to flip the catch –
as was their right – they'd find nada,
zilch, in the secret compartment.
They were all fishermen themselves –
they'd a Fish and Wildlife launch in dry dock
rigged with a swivel seat and its own livewell.
And he wanted to know who'd demand
he'd turn out three goodlength Choctaw bass
just to shine their torch in a vault he promised
held little of interest as Al Capone's.

There is a kind of crab known to devour human flesh.
There is a shelf five storeys undersea
Where small yachts pile up like bric-a-brac.
There is a town in Maryland called Alibi.

There is a layby on the lane between Uckfield
And Newhaven. There's a tendency
For roads which lead toward the coast to wheedle,
Flatter, like a streak of luck. And in reverse,

Of course, a countervailing tendency.
There is our fascination
With his vanishing, which is a way
To leave unbroached the business in the basement –

No, not quite. What's tasteless
Is to make his victim ballast for the fantasy.
There is a weight of water which
A scuttled boat might bear – midway

Across the English Channel, his
Takes that much then a little more
And tilts. There is a weight of guilt.
There is a parked car answering description somewhere.

## MANNERISMS

Won't come indoors, the tame deer.
Counts you out and in. Eats bread
from hand but not beseechingly.
Is haunted underhoof – by echo? –
on the patio. An expert otherwise
in sound-direction: raised voice
doesn't faze it, one turned syllable
will serve to dismiss. Watching
croquet from beyond the shadow line
of the leylandii once I caught it
cock its head to track the ball in motion.

## QUEBEC CITY

In the first stone house
on the American continent
I stood stone still
while our host whistled
up a tray of vol-au-vents,

and that was all which
passed from wall
to wall that day –
although the grey
American wind hauled

its whole unrolled half
hammered tarp across the roof,
and gave a show of
knowing full well
how things went in stone.

## LIGHTNING STRIKES SCHOOL TREE

No-one saw it but me and I had my eyes shut:
I'd given the class their Thomas Hardy worksheets,
the bell had gone off, hinging our double period,
everybody was scraping their chairs about,
there was an agreed low level of laugh and chat
and doubtless some thought was authentically
bent to the poem, some to the fizzy striplight,
some to the weight of the next forty minutes and some
to the far field out of the window
where – as I say – with my eyes shut
I saw not the flash but the mid-distance lime tree
pulled flat like the loop in a seam
at the fact of a needle: and then when I blinked
I could still see the needle, and I had my eyes shut.

First extricate your body, tardrop slow,
And pivot round to meet your interlocutor
Who now establishes in dreamy scattershot
Call-and-response that you are roughly who you
Say you are, full King (imposter souls
Slip down at this point, melding into sump
You're wobbling above), establisher
Of boundary stelae, mender of estate
And wildfowl net on newly profitable
Swampland, servant of the people – what you
Shy from here is any mention of the gods,
Whose shadows now you're starting to make out
Through what you took initially for swaying rushes:
The gods are wavering behind the rushes.

The gods are wavering behind the rushes:
Shifting their weight, unsettled, like the rushes
Whose shadows on the sand give this tribunal
Its atmosphere of justice done or underdone
Summarily, by soldiers far from home,
Who tear up nets, who billet on estates,
Who by night shift the boundary stelae over into
What's defensible (you're wobbling above
The bubble of the old souls on the hob
Shrieking *Imposter!*) – call yourself a King,
You'd better answer pronto this emissary –
Arsey emissary, pedantic weightsman, wight
You've swung around to see but find you now
Can't meet the eyes of, extricate your body –

## THE CUSPIS OF THE CONE

Every atom, Henry More decided,
was the almost-apex
of a cone turned upside-down
whose base was God
and point was Nothingness.
Our station was the very brink of Nothingness:
an angel falling down the cone
would steadily become more dense
until it apparated – if it overshot
presumably it burnt up, though
in practice God
had all of them on fishlines.
When His finger twitched
a fishline there were eight taut hierarchies
you could pop through: every time
you'd weigh a little less, or rather
more of you extruded
in the otherworld. Of people
(decently he mentioned plants as well)
only the faintest outline was extruded –
God (he didn't say this)
must have reckoned with us
more or less by guesswork. On the falling
spirits, he wrote: *these are they*
*which we handle and touch,*
*sufficient number compacted together.*
*Neither is the noise*
*of those small flies in a summer-evening*
*audible severally: but a full Quire of them*
*strike the ear with a pretty kind of buzzing.*

## MR KNOX'S HAMMOCK

I want to want to eat a little crow.
I want to feed the little crow crow back.
I want to cram raw crow down that crow's craw.
I want to sling a hammock down below.

If, say, I tie it to the mainmast stem
I want to still find rest when all the same
the sail fills with, haul!, the whole crew's roar.
It turns about the westwind, heaves a pall.

We're bound around the horn. We're bound to roar.
I want to stroke the crow that banged on deck.
I want to haul it skyward from my nest,
tensiled quid pro quo, of knots and air.

## CHILI BEAN SOUP

Done-ness of the onion
registers via no particular sense
as I push it round and round the pan.
Nor does it dawn
as awareness is supposed to,
that property sun
being winched by stagehands into consciousness.

We haven't verbs
for how we live through things,
our sensorium
coextensive with onion,
how we participate
at the scraping edge of the spatula. Nor would they help.
The channel's new-cut every time.

## NOTHING AFFIRMETH

Inside the sarcophagus lid
was a crib to the stars
in quicksilver
the dead king grinned up at.

And so he could read it
they'd floated a glim
on the sunken
lake of his chest,

which would gobble the oxygen
gutter and give out
and leave the stars
swaying:

the real stars, these ones.
He'd know when a meteor
scraped by
he'd husked his

sarcophagus carapace,
off he'd set sharpish,
a crib to the gods
was engraved on his cuff-bone.

The whole fen seemed on a tilt, at an angle of about five degrees on an axis orthogonal to the dyke path. It was dusk. Time and light were draining from the back of the landscape toward us. Over Ely, whose cathedral we could just make out on the horizon, it was almost midnight, and getting perceptibly darker. Where we were it was still warm, about six o'clock, the remnants of sunset lingered impossibly. All that moved was a small girl leading between stationary caravans her flock of named geese, whose daytime job was to crop the caravan lawns, heads cocked on one side scissoring grass an inch from ground level, not snatching it up in clumps like ruminants. We knew they were named because we heard her calling them, one by one, home over the cattle grid.

## TOUCH ME, TOUCH ME NOT

I broke the cobweb's guyline to the picture rail
realising too late I'd tripped a decoy

and the web's main body
had already pulled away, was drifting

on a microthermal to another ceiling corner.
Year's first bright day – streams

of light were keeping their bombardment up
and when one touched

the stretch of web it disappeared,
all but. Still standing on the chair I saw

another cobweb, wondered if
the two met would the tension of the first

be soft enough to untether
the other, would they cleave together, would

they wander through the flat
and snag what in their shared bright lines?

## THE SAME FROM THE AIR

Lane gets rounded off to
*lane* and field to *field*.
Someone's single-seater plane
hops over this particular
unmemorable ridge, then drops
a contour line. The wood's
a boundary case of what
you'd call a wood, a track
leads up to it but can't
get properly lost. It was
a wicked dodge to give
the motorway a number not
a not-quite-fitting name,
it was an abrogation of
our irresponsibility.
Real names we wrangle ready-
made until we round off
like the plane rounds off, to
chalk the short way home.

## THE REGIFT

In the back of the cave they stood around examining it.
I imagine them with torches which perhaps
they didn't need, for all I know the word *cave*
goes too deep. Read, any rock notch. It
was pillared, this skull, where a
stalactite and stalagmite had fused
and then the centre had been broken out.
A polar bear skull, much too central latitude.
A largish polar bear at that. They rapped
the braincase with their torch-butts
knocking any small gods off who might be still
adhering, photographed the skull in place
then walked back to the jeep then rode home with it.
I imagine it in someone's lap
being driven off the mountain, thumbs in both
eyesockets, how each time the jeep bangs curves
the sharpness of the bone swerves into consciousness:
and how each time the passenger (I see them
on the righthand backseat, bundled in
and then the skull's passed over) looks down
at their thickset obligation: past or just
below the engine's snarl-exhale, he or she
picks out, tap-tap, a little (I imagine) undertone.

## SALLY PURCELL CASHES UP AT THE KING'S ARMS

Turning over in her head a line of Charles d'Orleans
or last night's plausible ghost-sighting from a regular –
'on Little Clarendon Street, 3am
thin as a lamppost: zigzagging behind me,
keeping hidden: scared of being seen? detached itself
somewhere. At least by John Street I was certain that I'd lost it' –
turning over in her head also her way home, the advisability
of swapping for the pound that's in her bag
two 50ps the gas meter can swallow, Malory! that's who
the line was by. The counter-cache
for larger notes unlatches off a switch below the bar
and she transfers the lot to one mesh cashbag
with an irretrievable pressed seal. Chaucer
on the New Cross Road was robbed, he felt the lead goon's
razor-swizzel-stick against his gut and ponied up.
Bored undergraduates. Someone has left a wodge
of half-marked finals papers in a window seat,
she'll stick them in the safe too
with the coins (each one she's touched
on both sides, carefully, to count) and cheques and one abandoned
brilliant blue scarf. Sally Purcell! I'm cashing up myself.
I think of you fidgety in the barlight,
*gouttes d'argent d'orfèvrerie,* the five pence pieces
done, your straightener still umber in the optic,
and remembering the incline on the homestretch.

## AT HOUGHALL

After you have apportioned the bones
you will be made to restore the ox;
though cow parsley and nettletops
shine through faster than you'd expect

the toppled spoil. Where you walk
above the sealed portals, willow
farmed for garden furniture
teems into and excerpts the light.

That is, from heavy epic it
provides a manageable gloss
or makes a digest of the land.
But after you dole out the bones
they come round looking for the ox.

## A GENE SEQUENCE

What though my body run to dust?
Faith cleaves unto it, counting every grain,
With an exact and most particular trust,
Reserving all for flesh again.

George Herbert, 'Faith'

## START (CODON)

At the genomics conference I manned the desk,
Ticked off the names, wrote nametags, poured Buck's Fizz,
Gave everyone the abstracts on a USB and six stubs corresponding to
    their breakfasts.


## PHENYLALANINE

Thursday night's reception is a rubber sheet.
The reputations dropped on it are cannonballs of varying weight.
The postdocs orbiting are placed strategically to keep the big balls sweet.

Tray plucked of glasses, we can wheel
Through the staff wormhole,
Can watch the clusters form behind the conference room's dark-tinted
    one-way mirrorwall.


## LEUCINE

The part of boredom I like best
Takes up no room,
Adjusts no

Thermostat –
Threshold of interest,
Gorgeousness, rereadability –

Collapses no waveform,
Trips no alarm,
Tails off.

Coils up
The way a sundew
Coils up, the way a succulent

Conceals water, knuckles under
Thirsty pebbles,
Apprehensive,

Cupping its
Thin sap, until white
Gramophones erupt across the desert.


ISOLEUCINE

ASCII gibberish spews out across the backlit
Turquoise laminator interface that,
Try who might, will not display its fault –

A choice of three – Wrong Paper Setting /
Trapped Pocket in Rollers / Overheating.
Can't reset without the fault in writing.

And who was it in seven-segment typefaces
Taught Caliban a language with no curses?
Allowed our things to bootstrap on our voices?


TYROSINE

Tired last night we left our long-deferred conversation
Ajar, having made small
Tentative soundings of one another –

The word now, *child*, unrescindable,
Already fleshing out,
Carving the world-gap where its name will go.


## METHIONINE

At the genomics conference I managed the uploads,
Teched for the parallel sessions, followed SCART leads
Gripfixed under backboards to a single dusty arm-thick motherlode.


## VALINE

Grass smutched between
The wheel and the wheel nut of our
Tea trolley. On the lawn

Great Horned Owls soar
Turn in the air and drop and grip,
Claw shyly at the falconer's

Glove, in a pseudo-swoop
Throw open their big wings like fire doors
Are opened when the session stops.

Gleams of applause –
The session slightly overran –
Grow and fall back. The doors. The owls are there for three more hours.

## SERINE

This not-quite-soundproofing
Converts the plenary
To just pitch    Rise and fall

Tacking through fog
Count flashlight pips
Chirrups on GPS

Thrum of the argument
Coasting a sandbar here
A jab of light

Throws for an instant every
Cove and inlet open
Golden    Suddenly negotiable


## HISTIDINE

Conversation in bed now picks round at our one un
Avoidable
Topic, trying to weigh how it's tethered,

Checks off each possible tone as in
Adequate,
Compromised, somebody's already thwarted approach road –


## PROLINE

Closer for the fire door de
Couples from its magnet pad
Then like a certain time of day –

Call it, the time before you say you're
Coming off your break, and add
Conditions exponentially:

Come back via the scenic way,
Come carrying the sense you had
An inkling of, that easy joy –

Collapses like thumbprinted dough.
Come back. It closes with a thud.
Grabs tightly, like security.


THREONINE

A single test tube stopper like a snapped high heel;
Cylinders of different volumes; Erlenmeyer flasks; an oddball
Test tube rack, hardwood with wire inlay and about as stable

As this much-too-high-up teeter-totter shelf is stable;
Crater-walls of dust and dust in ramparts, cornmeal-
Coloured, I must sift through, standing on a stool stood on a table;

Alembic; burette in corroded steel
Clamp; ziploc of kibble;
A flask blowing a smaller flask as bubble;

Accumulation of the last long while,
Cupboards, file cases, high shelves full;
Get gone, your hunt's in vain, the keys were lost, the boxes went
    unlabelled.

## ALANINE

Gnarly q&a, the speaker over-
Confrontational, the roving mic
Too quiet then too tremolo.

Good session though for kvetching over
Coffee at; they spill into the break,
Consensus is, it blows. Their

Gossip shimmers, just the rhythm
Caught: its lovely modulations, amic-
Able sham-withdrawal

Give-and-take, catch-as-catch-
Can – even the accents of complaint are
Gossamer, are mediated tremolo.


## GLUTAMINE

Conversation the next day
Adjoins our one topic, transitions
Abruptly to dodge the particulars you say

Convinced you: suppose the world stays
As it is, our positions
Grow airier, bite the breeze, billow away?

## ASPARAGINE

Admin; the dust was endless; I inserted
Alternately drawing pins and certain small red pegs
Trifold display boards need to keep their feet

Aligned, for Friday's poster session; I converted
.ai files into .jpegs;
*Child, my child.* I dreamed that I was dancing in the street.


## GLUTAMIC ACID

Giddy from the plenary's wise handling of the last Q of the Q&
A,
Among the attendees of our penultimate icebreaker (Saturday)

Gaggles of postdocs recapitulate among themselves the fluent
A,
Gliding from sass to effortlessly modulated '...Anyway –'


## CYSTEINE

Together we head down to the refectory.
Grab sandwiches. Sit outside on the grass.
The birds of prey display was yesterday.

The birds of prey display was yesterday.
Grab sandwiches. Grab vapour-trailed sky.
Claws out and snatch. And caught. And does not pass.

## TRYPTOPHAN

Tat we load into the party totes: all branded:
GlaxoSmithKline worryballs, Rockland Immunochemicals with
Gummy cowskulls advertising bovine serum albumin –


## ARGININE

Conference dissipates after a light lunch.
Goes to the Man on
The Moon as it's close to the station.

Calls or gets us to call for a taxi.
Goes for an un
Called-for after-lunch dram at the Mitre.

Checks out of airbnb or youth hostel or
Guest accommodation
At college and heads straightaway to the Panton Arms.

Cold collation for lunch; and we're welcome to
Graze on any scran
Going, before we shepherd off lingering

Attendees to the Elm Tree, Cambridge Blue,
Granta or Baron
According to whim of the dogsbody;

After which conference actually dissipates:
Greater Anglia to London,
Govia Thameslink back north to the eastward changes.

## SERINE

Awake last night we sat up and spoke for a while,
Granted each other finally points which the other was
Taking for granted, and everything in our rickety

Answer stayed upright still: taking the world as a
Given; each other as given; our wobbly pivot as given.
Child, it's taken all for a given, and yours for the taking.


## GLYCINE

| | |
|---|---|
| Gone: burnt dust reek from the OHP. | *Get* |
| Getting gone: the final guests | *Gone* |
| That pace outside the admin office singly. | *Thymine* |
| | |
| Gone: email questionnaire with no attachment. | *Get* |
| Getting gone: the rough gist | *Gone* |
| Conference proceedings, as yet unsent. | *Cytosine* |
| | |
| Gone: the trestle tables and name badges. | *Get* |
| Getting gone: unguessed- | *Gone* |
| At small connections round the edges. | *Adenine* |
| | |
| Gone: gone home, gone quiet, gone to seed. | *Get* |
| Getting gone: us and the ghosts. | *Gone* |
| Gather them up. Set fob alarm. Bid godspeed. | *Guanine* |

## STOP (CODA)

That said let's you and I slope off
And half-knowing where we're headed to
Arrive at some ungodly hour

Torchlit old-style hacienda
Abutting a desert garden
Gathering across which stride

Tall green simultaneously-flowering cacti
Grown from love, love's basic
Admin, love's rich days of busywork.

## ON THE RED-EYE

Caribou the starving wolf
had chased half-heartedly
obtained a blind crevasse
took stock and turned. A male
dragged his chandelier of antlers
through the snow to demarcate
the ground he'd stand.

The wolf had burnt her
entire winterstock of fat
already, next to go
would be the layer round her heart.
She'd cycled through her tactics
and her fallback tactics. She had
no clue what she'd do.

Above them, on the red-eye,
someone dreamt they were
the only passenger awake
and woke to find it true,
or true depending
on how deep sleep has to be
before you call it sleep.

*Epigraph*
From Robert Thorndike's review in the *American Educational Research Journal*, 5(4), 1968, of *Pygmalion in the Classroom* by Robert Rosenthal and Lenore Jacobson.

*'The Sun Box'*
The French materials scientist and Nobel laureate, Pierre-Gilles de Gennes, asked about the prospects for viable nuclear fusion reactors, replied 'We say that we will put the sun into a box. The idea is pretty. The problem is, we don't know how to make the box.'

*'A Gene Sequence'*
The genetic code is the language of our DNA. It encodes the instructions for making proteins, the working parts of our cells. Each protein is a chain of amino acids; the DNA sequence specifies the order in which the amino acids are assembled, and the genetic code is the language of that specification. Three nucleotides – repeated blocks of DNA – form the unit which translates into one amino acid. There are four kinds of nucleotide, Adenine, Thymine, Guanine and Cytosine, abbreviated to A, T, G and C, and each amino acid is specified by several nucleotide triplets – for instance, the amino acid phenylalanine is encoded by both T,T,T and T,T,C. There are also triplets which encode instructions to begin and end an individual protein.

'A Gene Sequence' takes the abbreviations of the nucleotide triplets as initial letters of each line; the individual sections are named after the amino acids being coded; the narrative takes place in Cambridge, on the Biomedical Campus at the end of Hills Road, post-Brexit and pre-pandemic.

## ACKNOWLEDGEMENTS

Emily napped while I was writing, and when she woke up she was indulgent when I read her what I'd written.

I'm grateful to Daphne Astor, James Brookes, Will Burns, Adam Crothers, Katy Evans-Bush, Dai George, David Harsent, Marius Kociejowski, Maureen McLane, Sam Quill, Patrick Davidson Roberts, Ben Rogers, Dec Ryan, Anna Selby, Robert Selby, Martha Sprackland, Claudine Toutoungi, Rebecca Watts, Joe Williams, James Womack and Alex Wong, for advice and encouragement.

Some of these poems have been previously published in *PN Review*, *The World Speaking Back* (Boiler House Press, 2018), *Pinecoast* (Hazel Press, 2021), and broadcast on BBC Radio Cambridgeshire. 'The Lecture Notes' was written for S.J. Fowler's 'Enemies' project.

Thank you also to Eli Lischka for her help with the Spanish, to Sarah for reminding me of what and how much looks the same from the air, and to everyone at the LRB Bookshop and Carcanet Press.